D0603170

ABOVE AND BEYOND

WITH

CREATIVITY AND INNOVATION

ROBIN JOHNSON

Crabtree Publishing Company
www.crabtreebooks.com

Author: Robin Johnson

Series research and development: Reagan Miller

Editors: Sonya Newland, Kathy Middleton, and Janine Deschenes

Proofreader: Kelly Spence

Designer: Rocket Design Ltd

Photo researchers: Robin Johnson and Sonya Newland

Cover design: Katherine Berti

Production coordinator and prepress technician: Tammy McGarr

Print coordinator: Katherine Berti

Produced for Crabtree Publishing by White-Thomson Publishing

Photographs:
Alamy: Noiro: p. 9b, Byron Motley: p. 33t, Lebrecht Music and Arts Photo Library: p. 36b; Rocket Design: p. 15, p. 41b, p. 43t; Shutterstock: MR.LIGHTMAN1975: p. 1, EKS: p. 4b, Chamille White: pp. 6–7, krsmanovic: p. 8, rzymuR: p. 9t, Ollyy: p. 10, p. 25, Kalakruthi: p. 11t, Yuriy Rudyy: p. 12b, rvlsoft: p. 13t, p. 44(3), Creativa Images: p. 13b, Titima Ongkantong: p. 14, art4all: p. 16t, MagMac83: p. 16b, Jamie Wilson: p. 17, gst: p. 18t, p. 26b, Photobac: p. 18b, abstract: p. 19, Rawpixel.com: p. 20, Avesun: p. 22, Titima Ongkantong: p. 21, Anky: p. 23, Antonio Guillem: p. 24, Digital Storm: p. 26t, nelik: p. 29t, mtmmarek: p. 29b, inefotostudio: pp. 30–31, Peppinuzzo: p. 31t, vesna cvorovic: p. 32, Helder Almeida: p. 34l, lipik: p. 34r, Dragon Images: p. 35t, MSSA: p. 35b, browndogstudios: p. 36t, Gil C: p. 37t, Andy Frith: p. 37b, Jovanovic Dejan: p. 38, Laralova: p. 39, vectorEps10: p. 40, Taina Sohlman: p. 41t, p. 42: Myimagine, Antikwar: p. 44(1), EM Arts: p. 44(2), Rose Carson: p. 44(4), digitalreflections: p. 44(5), Zeynep Demir: p. 44(6), Pixel Embargo: p. 44(7), Costazzurra: p. 45, Esteban De Armas: p. 45; Stefan Chabluk: p. 6b, p. 7b, p. 11b, p. 12t, p. 33b, p. 43b.

All other images by Shutterstock

Library and Archives Canada Cataloguing in Publication

Johnson, Robin (Robin R.), author
    Above and beyond with creativity and innovation / Robin Johnson.

(Fueling your future! going above and beyond in the 21st century)
Includes index.
Issued in print and electronic formats.
ISBN 978-0-7787-2831-3 (hardback).--
ISBN 978-0-7787-2845-0 (paperback).--
ISBN 978-1-4271-1835-6 (html)

    1. Creative thinking--Juvenile literature. 2. Creative ability--Juvenile literature. I. Title.

BF408.J63 2016   j153.3'5   C2016-903307-4
                                          C2016-903308-2

Library of Congress Cataloging-in-Publication Data

CIP available at the Library of Congress

Crabtree Publishing Company
www.crabtreebooks.com   1-800-387-7650

Printed in Canada/082016/TL20160715

Published in Canada
Crabtree Publishing
616 Welland Ave.
St. Catharines, Ontario
L2M 5V6

Published in the United States
Crabtree Publishing
PMB 59051
350 Fifth Avenue, 59th Floor
New York, New York 10118

Published in the United Kingdom
Crabtree Publishing
Maritime House
Basin Road North, Hove
BN41 1WR

Published in Australia
Crabtree Publishing
3 Charles Street
Coburg North
VIC, 3058

CONTENTS

CHAPTER ONE

THE CREATIVE SPIRIT

Creativity and Innovation

Creativity is the ability to come up with ideas that are original and useful. It involves thinking in ways that are not usual or expected, using your **imagination**, and connecting ideas and objects in new ways. Getting creative means looking at problems from all angles, asking questions, and coming up with unique solutions.

Innovation is the act of creating something new by making improvements or changes to a product or process in order to solve a problem. It involves putting creative ideas into action and trying new approaches to get things done. Creativity and innovation are closely linked. Innovators need creative ideas to put in motion, and innovations—from paintbrushes to smartphones—allow people to express their creativity.

Critical thinking

Collaboration

Creavity

Communication

Are You a Creative Genius?

What do you know about creativity and innovation? The following are some things you may have heard or thought. Do you agree with them?

1. Creativity is only useful for producing paintings, music, and other types of art.

2. You can recognize innovators by their crazy hair and lab coats.

3. Everything that can be invented has already been invented.

4. You are either born creative or you never will be.

None of these statements are true, of course. The following statements paint a better picture of creativity and innovation today.

1. Creativity is useful in all areas of life, including school, home, work, and when you pursue your interests.

2. Innovative people are everywhere, in all walks of life and doing all sorts of jobs.

3. There is no end to innovation. New things are constantly being created.

4. Creativity is a skill that you can learn, practice, and improve.

> "If you can dream it, you can do it."
>
> *Walt Disney,* who called the creative people who designed his theme parks "imagineers"

21st Century Skills

Our digitally interconnected world is always changing and evolving. To keep up and be successful, we have to be lifelong learners, which means that we must be constantly learning how to think in new and innovative ways. The Partnership for 21st Century Learning is an organization that has identified four essential skills that students need to build to achieve their goals at school, at work, and in their personal lives. They are the 4Cs—communication, collaboration, **creativity**, and critical thinking. Each skill is important on its own, but combining the four together in our everyday lives is the key to success in a 21st century world!

Born This Way

People are creative by nature. As a toddler, you may have built upside-down cities, made up crazy dances, colored outside the lines, or expressed yourself in other creative ways. Later, you learned how to follow rules and instructions. You may have been told that there was only one "right" answer to a problem. You may have stifled your creative impulses to make friends and get good grades. Before long, you were probably building cities the right way up, dancing the way all your friends do, and coloring inside the lines.

Why Be Creative?

You might think that creativity is only important to people such as artists or writers, but people use creative-thinking skills to meet important needs and solve all kinds of complex problems. In the past, creative thinkers came up with ideas that solved straightforward problems, and had clear goals. People needed a way of harnessing electricity for light, so Thomas Edison developed the lightbulb. There was no way to travel long distances quickly, so the Wright brothers invented the airplane.

Today, people use creative-thinking skills in all aspects of their lives—at home, school, work, and in social settings—and to solve 21st century problems that don't always have simple solutions. Scientists search for cures to the common cold and rare diseases. Engineers design new technologies that improve our lives. Students make music videos and 3D models—and come up with creative excuses for why their homework is not done!

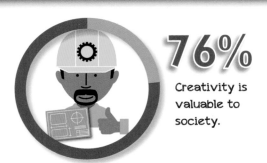

76% Creativity is valuable to society.

75% Creativity is important personally.

In a survey of 1,000 American adults, three-quarters felt that creativity was valuable and important.

Express Yourself

People also use creativity to express their thoughts and feelings, and to connect with others. They paint pictures, write poems, and make music that show how they feel and offer interpretations of the world around them. They design creative cakes and outrageous outfits and innovative buildings to show the world their unique style. Sometimes this means that you have to "unlearn" the rules and think outside the box.

> ## "Every child is an artist. The problem is how to remain an artist once he grows up."
> ### *Pablo Picasso*

Make It Your Own

How do you think your own creativity compares to the results shown in this study? Explain why you are more or less creative now than when you were five years old.

Creative Geniuses

Research shows that creativity peaks at the age of five. In one study, 1,600 five-year-old children were given a NASA creativity test—a test used to find innovative scientists and engineers. Nearly all the children scored as creative geniuses. The same children were tested at the ages of 10 and 15, and their scores dropped dramatically. Only two percent of the 280,000 adults tested scored at the creative genius level.

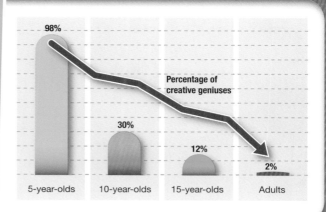

Percentage of creative geniuses

	98%	30%	12%	2%
	5-year-olds	10-year-olds	15-year-olds	Adults

CHAPTER TWO

MAKING HISTORY

The Wheels Are Turning

People have always created and innovated to meet their needs and solve their problems. The wheel was one of the first great innovations. It was invented in Mesopotamia around 3500 B.C.E. and was first used to make pottery. It was not until 300 years later, however, that some creative person thought to use it in a different way—as a wooden wheel on a cart—and really got things rolling.

The invention of the wheel got the show on the road!

Art Imitates Life

Most ancient cultures did not view wheels or other innovations as acts of creation. That means they felt the wheel had already been created by the gods, and they had simply discovered it. They believed that people could imitate life, but they could not create anything new; only gods had the power to do that. Ancient Roman and Greek artists looked to the Muses for inspiration—the goddesses in mythology who inspired art, literature, and science. Today, people use the term "muse" to refer to someone who inspires them to be creative, and the word "museum" is derived from that word.

Renaissance Men and Women

Ideas about creativity did not change until a period in the 1500s called the Renaissance in Europe. During that period, there was new interest in art, science, architecture, and literature. The work of individual creators and innovators began to be valued. Painters such as Leonardo da Vinci and Michelangelo became famous as artists, but they also invented machines, wrote poetry, studied mathematics, and figured out how the body works. The work of creative women, such as the Italian painter Sofonisba Anguissola, also began to be recognized during this period.

Renaissance Man

Leonardo da Vinci was the original "Renaissance man." Today we use the term Renaissance man or woman to describe someone who is interested in and knows a lot about many things. Da Vinci was a painter, sculptor, architect, scientist, engineer, and inventor—an all-around creative genius.

Revolutionary Ideas

During the Industrial Revolution, people began to harness their creativity. New inventions, such as the steam engine, made work easier and allowed factories to produce the items people needed much faster, and in huge quantities. This is called **mass production**. There was new focus on innovation and its power to make money. Later inventions, such as the lightbulb and the automobile, were successful only if they could be mass produced.

Da Vinci combined mathematics and art in his drawing titled *Vitruvian Man*.

> **"Genius is 1 percent inspiration and 99 percent perspiration."**
> *Thomas Edison*

SPOTLIGHT

In 1879, Thomas Edison invented the first practical electric lightbulb. Other inventors had created lightbulbs before, but the bulbs did not last long, or they used materials such as platinum **filaments** that made them very expensive to mass produce. Edison set out to shed some light on the problem. He and his team studied the designs of earlier lightbulbs and tried to improve them. They tested thousands of theories until Edison came up with the bright idea of using bamboo inside a bulb. His idea worked and his invention became a shining success. Today, we call a spark of creativity a "lightbulb moment."

Putting It to the Test

In the 1950s, people began to view creativity as a skill that could be learned and improved through practice. American psychologist J.P. Guilford believed that the basis of creativity was the ability to come up with multiple solutions to a problem. He called that ability "**divergent thinking**." The word "divergent" means "moving away from what is expected." Guilford invented tests that measured divergent-thinking skills. For example, Guilford's Alternative Uses Task asks participants to list as many possible uses for everyday objects as they can in a set amount of time.

The Father of Creativity

Building on Guilford's work, Dr. E. Paul Torrance set out to prove that being creative was just as important as being smart—and that creativity could be measured the way IQ tests measure intelligence. In 1966, he invented the Torrance Tests of Creative Thinking. The tests ask students to complete pictures, imagine stories, predict outcomes, and perform other writing and drawing tasks. Tests are scored on the number and originality of answers, how many different areas the answers cover, and the amount of detail given. The Torrance Tests have been taken by millions of people and been translated into more than 50 languages. They are still widely used in schools—particularly for identifying **gifted** students—and by companies around the world, which give the tests during interviews to make sure they hire the most creative people.

This old-school challenge will have you thinking divergently.

Materials needed:

Pen and paper, stopwatch

Challenge:

Pick an everyday object, such as a paper clip, brick, or spoon. List as many uncommon or unusual uses for the object as you can in three minutes. Compare your ideas with a friend's list, then **collaborate** to see if you can come up with even more ideas.

In the Torrance Tests of Creative Thinking, students are asked to finish incomplete figures in creative ways. How would you complete the drawings on the left?

Make It Your Own

Have you ever taken a creativity test in school? Do you think tests are an accurate way to measure a person's creativity? Explain your thinking.

Creativity Today

Today, there is a great need for creative-thinking skills. Digital technologies demand our attention and creativity, whether we are designing virtual worlds and avatars to inhabit them, making videos that go viral on YouTube, posting original pictures on Instagram, or expressing ourselves creatively in blogs and on social media. Companies race to design smaller and smarter phones, greener electric cars, cooler running shoes, and other products that they hope will improve people's lives. And scientists, engineers, and other innovators make our technology-driven world spin even faster.

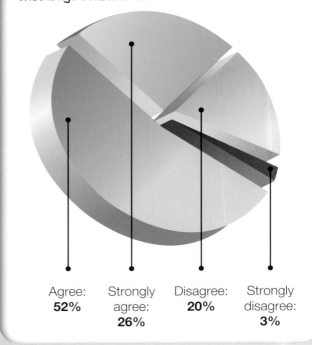

More than three-quarters of American teachers believe that today's digital technologies encourage students to be more creative.

Agree: **52%** Strongly agree: **26%** Disagree: **20%** Strongly disagree: **3%**

Watch for Falling Creativity

Although creativity is important, we seem to be getting less and less creative. A recent study analyzed nearly 300,000 Torrance Tests taken by American school-aged children and adults over the last 40 years. Creativity scores rose steadily until 1990, but since then the scores have been dropping. No one really knows the reasons why. Many people think it has to do with the popularity of electronic devices and the invention of the Internet. Young people today spend more time on these devices and less time reading and playing outdoors than they did in the past. They have less free, unscheduled time to let their minds wander and build their creative-thinking skills. They are rarely bored—and it is boredom that often forces people to get creative and make their own fun.

The Good News

The good news is that falling creativity scores can be turned around. Anyone can learn how to be a creative thinker and innovator. You can practice divergent thinking to generate bright ideas. You can follow a creative process (see page 15) to improve your creative-thinking skills. You can learn how to be creative again—and must do so in order to succeed in the 21st century.

facebook

Today, there's a new breed of Renaissance men and women. Innovators like Facebook cofounder Mark Zuckerberg are changing the face of technology.

Make It Your Own

Today, movie magic is not reserved for Hollywood producers. In fact, there are 300 hours of new videos uploaded to YouTube every minute! Have you ever posted a video for YouTube? How did you put your own creative spin on it to make it stand out from the crowd? If making videos isn't for you, think about the qualities of the YouTube videos that stand out to you!

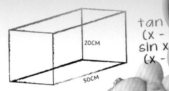

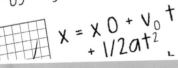

Genius Hours

Some teachers today are making time for **genius hours** in their classrooms—periods in which students can get creative and think outside their textbooks. Students choose their own topics, ask questions about them, conduct in-depth research, and later share what they have learned.

CHAPTER THREE

THE CREATIVE PROCESS

Great Minds Think Alike

Have you heard the saying "great minds think alike"? Creative people definitely do not think alike, but they do follow a similar creative process. They also share certain personality traits. Creative people are…

Curious
They question everything they know—or think they know—about the world. They wonder why and how things happen.

Hardworking
They roll up their sleeves and get dirty, putting in long hours and sometimes years of hard work before inspiration strikes.

Passionate
They have strong feelings or beliefs about what they're doing, whether they're making a statue or a scientific breakthrough.

Observant
They pay attention to even the smallest details—which allows them to make unexpected connections when they're painting the big picture.

Fearless
They are not afraid to take risks or to fail—often again and again—in the pursuit of creative genius.

Persistent
They keep trying to find solutions. They don't see failure as a setback, but rather as an opportunity to learn.

Flexible
They are open to change and willing to experiment with new things. If something doesn't work, they go back to the drawing board and try again.

Make It Your Own
Look at the information on this page. Which characteristics do you possess? Which ones could you work on to improve your creative-thinking skills?

How Does Creativity Happen?

Most people think creativity happens in an instant. You have a "lightbulb moment" and suddenly get a brilliant idea. But creativity is a process that takes work. No one knows for sure how that process happens, but some very creative people have come up with theories about the creative process. In 1926, a psychologist named Graham Wallas developed a four-step theory, based on his own research and the accounts, or experiences, of inventors and other famously creative people. His theory is still widely used and is a model in this chapter.

Step by Step

Wallas outlined four stages in the creative process: preparation, **incubation**, **illumination**, and **verification**. The process begins with lots of preparation. You define the problem, gather information, set limits, and generate ideas. Then you step away from the problem and let it stew for a while. This is the incubation period, when you turn the information over in your mind, and start to form ideas. The illumination stage is when your best idea takes shape in your mind. This could be your own "lightbulb moment." Finally, you examine your idea critically to verify, or make sure, it is an effective solution, then **refine** it and **elaborate** on it. Each step of the creative process will be explained in more detail in this chapter.

THE 4 STAGES
OF THE
CREATIVE PROCESS
1   2   3   4
Preparation   Incubation   Illumination   Verification

Step 1: Preparation

In the first step of the creative process, you focus your mind on a problem and prepare to get creative. You gather information and learn as much as you can about the problem. This step can take minutes, days, weeks, or even years to complete. It is an essential step that is often overlooked in the rush to create and innovate. But the better prepared you are, the more effective the creative process will be.

What's Your Problem?

Start by clearly defining the need you want to meet or the problem you want to solve. Try writing the problem down on a piece of paper or on the computer. Ask yourself why the problem is happening. When you have come up with around five reasons, or "whys," you will probably be able to reach the root of your problem. For example, when Thomas Edison was preparing to design a lightbulb, he could have made a "five whys" chart like this:

Problem: The design of the lightbulb needs to be improved.

Why? — Because the lightbulb doesn't last long enough.

Why? — Because the filament inside the bulb burns too quickly.

Why? — Because there is too much heat inside the bulb and the filament can't withstand it.

Why? — Because the filament isn't made of a heat-resistant material.

Why? — Because an affordable, heat-resistant material hasn't been discovered yet.

So the root of one of Edison's problems was that he needed to find an affordable, long-lasting, heat-resistant material to use for the filament inside the lightbulb.

Lay the Groundwork

Once you have defined your problem, you can start gathering information. Do some research to see if a solution already exists. If it does, you can change or build on it in a creative way. If it does not, the research will lay the groundwork for some new, innovative solutions of your own. Before you start generating ideas, however, you need to establish some **criteria** for your solution. This is key to keeping the creative process on track so that your solution effectively solves your problem. For example, the criteria for the electric lightbulb might be that it must be safe, long-lasting, and inexpensive to mass produce.

SPOTLIGHT

Eesha Khare's cell phone always needed to be recharged, so the 18-year-old student answered the call and found a solution. She spent a year researching and learning about existing charging technologies. Then she found a way to improve a device called a "supercapacitor." In 2013, Khare invented a portable device that can charge a cell phone in less than 30 seconds instead of the hours it usually takes.

"If I had an hour to solve a problem I'd spend 55 minutes thinking about the problem and five minutes thinking about solutions."

Albert Einstein

17

Get Divergent

Once you've laid the groundwork for the creative process, you can start to get divergent. Divergent thinking uses your memory and experiences to come up with many unique answers to open-ended questions. Open-ended questions are ones that require more than yes, no, or other one-word answers. They have many possible answers. For example, "How can I make a lightbulb more energy-efficient?" is an open-ended question. Just like there are many solutions to every problem, there are many strategies to practice and improve your divergent-thinking skills.

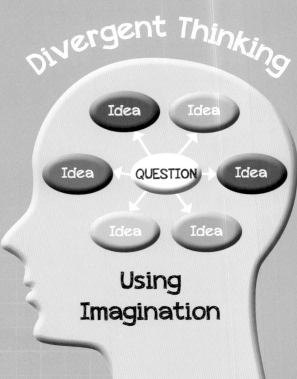

Divergent Thinking

Idea · Idea · Idea · QUESTION · Idea · Idea · Idea

Using Imagination

Role-Playing

This strategy gets you acting—and thinking—like someone else. Pretend you're a deep-sea diver, a tightrope walker, or anyone else you can imagine. Then consider how they would interpret the question and what skills and life experiences they might bring to the table. For example, a deep-sea diver might try using seaweed inside a lightbulb. A tightrope walker might suggest using wire from his tightrope act.

Free-Writing

Free-writing is a strategy that helps free up your creativity. Start writing and don't stop until the time is up (usually 5 to 15 minutes). Don't worry about punctuation, spelling mistakes, or going off topic. Just let the ideas flow freely from one to another. For example, the lightbulb topic might lead to the sun…which might lead to a garden…which might lead to a salad…which might make you think about lunch…and what your lunch is wrapped in may give you the idea to try aluminum foil inside a lightbulb.

Reverse Thinking

This strategy gets you thinking backward to move the creative process forward. Write down a problem statement, then restate it in reverse to see it in a whole new light. For example, a problem such as "How could a lightbulb use less energy?" might become "How could a lightbulb use more energy?" List possible solutions to the new problem. For example, you could keep the lights on when you leave a room. Then reverse the solutions to help solve your original problem. Lights that turn off automatically when you leave a room would use less energy.

HANDS ON

Combining objects and ideas in unexpected ways is key to divergent thinking—and this activity will have you doing just that.

Materials needed:
Pen and paper

Challenge:
To begin, divide a piece of paper into three columns. List random objects in the first two columns. Then combine the objects to come up with some new inventions and record them in the third column. Keep changing the combinations to come up with bigger and better innovations.

Objects	Objects	Innovations
umbrella	flashlight	An umbrella with a built-in flashlight for rainy nights
clock	toothbrush	A toothbrush with a timer to make sure you brush long enough
chair	skis	A wheelchair on skis that can travel through snow

Brainstorming

Brainstorming is one of the best ways to help you start thinking divergently. Brainstorming involves asking a question and then quickly listing all the answers you can think of—even those that seem impractical or impossible. This type of divergent thinking can be done alone or in a group. Brainstorming with others often generates more ideas because diverse groups bring different memories and experiences to the table. Other people's ideas can also spark your own creativity. Try the strategies on this page to get your mind racing and your brain storming.

Square-Pegging

Have you ever heard the phrase, "You can't fit a square peg in a round hole"? Square-pegging is a way of thinking that gets you looking at objects and ideas in a new light. Start by thinking of ways your object could do things that it is not intended to do, then try to come up with as many creative answers as you can to fit that "square peg" into a "round hole." For example, how could a lightbulb win a beauty pageant? A contestant could design a creative outfit with a lightbulb hat that earns him the crown. Or a lightbulb could burn out in the dressing room and cause the frontrunner to trip and fall in the dark.

SCAMPER

This strategy uses the acronym **SCAMPER** to get you brainstorming questions and answers. The words that make up the acronym and some sample questions are shown below.

SUBSTITUTE: What materials could you substitute for glass or other lightbulb parts?

COMBINE: What would happen if you combined a lightbulb with another innovation?

ADAPT: How could you adapt the lightbulb to serve another use?

MODIFY: How could you change the shape or look of the lightbulb?

PUT TO ANOTHER USE: Could the lightbulb be used for something else besides making light?

ELIMINATE: What could you remove from the lightbulb to make it better?

REVERSE: What would happen if you reversed the flow of electricity in the lightbulb?

This challenge will get you "thinking small" to help you generate big ideas. When you set limits—such as time, money, materials, or words—it forces you to look at a problem in new ways.

Materials needed:
Pen and paper or computer

Challenge:
Dr. Seuss wrote *Green Eggs and Ham* after his publisher bet him he couldn't write a book using just 50 different words. Use those words—shown below—to create an original poem or short story. You can write it in a house. You can write it with a mouse. You can write it here or there. You can write it anywhere!

a, am, and, anywhere, are, be, boat, box, car, could, dark, do, eat, eggs, fox, goat, good, green, ham, here, house, I, if, in, let, like, may, me, mouse, not, on, or, rain, Sam, say, see, so, thank, that, the, them, there, they, train, tree, try, will, with, would, you

Try These!
Follow these four brainstorming guidelines to get the bright ideas going lightning fast.

> "The best way to have a good idea is to have lots of ideas."
> *Scientist Linus Pauling*

The more ideas you generate, the better your chances of finding a solution.

Don't put down anyone's ideas at this stage. You can evaluate and critique later.

Let your creativity run wild and try to look at things in new ways.

Combine and build on other people's ideas to come up with more solutions.

Go big **Let it go** **Go wild** **Go together**

Step 2: Incubation

In the incubation stage of the creative process, you step back from the problem for a while. You stop actively looking for an answer and, instead, think about other things so that the information in your mind can settle and mix together. Sometimes, preparing and brainstorming doesn't help you come up with your brightest idea right away. The best way to find a creative solution could be to stop looking for it and let your mind rest.

"All truly great thoughts are conceived while walking."

Philosopher Friedrich Nietzsche

Of Two Minds

Some scientists believe that the human mind is made up of two parts—the **conscious** and **subconscious**. The conscious is the part of the mind we are aware of. It uses the five senses to observe the world around us, analyze our observations, and make decisions. You are using the conscious part of your mind to read and understand this book. The subconscious is the part of the mind that we are not aware of. It stores all our thoughts, feelings, and memories. It combines ideas and makes new connections based on our past experiences and stored knowledge. The subconscious continues to generate creative ideas and solve problems even after we have moved on to other tasks. Right now your subconscious may be working on ideas for a song or a science-fair project.

Give It a Rest

In the incubation stage, let your mind wander and think about other things, or don't think about anything at all. When the conscious part of your mind is not focused on a task, your subconscious can step up and get creative. Simple, mindless activities—such as taking a shower, exercising, or playing ping-pong—give your brain a break and let your creative juices flow. Napping is another easy but effective way to put your problems to bed. Your subconscious works overtime while you're asleep, and often you'll dream up a solution or wake up with a creative idea.

Hold the Key

Artist Salvador Dalí found that short power naps were key to his creative success. The Spanish painter rested in a chair with a metal key in his hand. The key would drop and wake him as soon as he fell asleep—but by then inspiration had already struck. Dalí's art often had a dreamlike quality.

SPOTLIGHT

Dmitri Mendeleev was a Russian chemist and inventor who brought his creativity to the table. In 1869, he struggled to find a suitable way to organize the **chemical elements**. He spent months searching for patterns and trends. Then one day, he fell asleep at his desk and his subconscious struck gold. Mendeleev dreamed up the periodic table, a grid that groups elements based on their **properties** and allows scientists to predict at a glance how chemicals will react with each other.

Step 3: Illumination

You get your bright ideas in the illumination stage of the creative process. After careful preparation and plenty of incubation, this stage of the creative process is usually brief. Your subconscious has been working away, combining ideas and making connections. You may have a sudden idea or "lightbulb moment." Or, many ideas might start coming together in your mind, helping you to develop a great solution.

Rush to the Head

You can't force illumination or control how it occurs. Sometimes ideas come to you in bits and pieces. You wake up with part of a solution, then think about the problem some more and develop the idea further. Other times, the idea is fully formed in your mind and ready to be put to the test. You also can't control where or when illumination happens. English physicist and mathematician Sir Isaac Newton was drinking tea in his garden when a falling apple sparked his creativity and helped him formulate the law of gravity.

Light It Up

Follow these tips to catch your inspiration—
wherever and whenever it hits!

- **Keep an open mind** and be ready to receive any ideas that pop into your brain—even if they aren't perfect or don't make sense right away. Your subconscious will keep giving you pieces of the puzzle until it all fits together.

- **Write down all your ideas**. Carry a notebook or cell phone to record your thoughts on the go. If you don't have one when inspiration strikes, you could borrow a friend's phone and send yourself a voice message or text. Or, write down your ideas on a napkin!

- **Keep a pen and notebook beside your bed**. You might wake up in the middle of the night with a great idea—and it might be gone in the morning if you don't jot it down.

- **Don't ignore a bright idea** or push it aside until later, because often it won't be there when you want it. There is nothing more frustrating than finally getting the solution you've been waiting for and then quickly forgetting it.

SPOTLIGHT

Archimedes was a famous scientist and mathematician in ancient Greece who found illumination in a bathtub. The story goes that he had been puzzling over how to calculate the **volume** of irregular-shaped objects. When he stuck his leg into the bathtub, he saw that the water level rose. He suddenly realized that an object placed under water—whatever its shape—would displace, or move, an amount of water equal to the object's volume, just like his leg did. Archimedes leapt out of the tub and shouted "Eureka!" (which means "I have found it" in Greek). He was so excited about his idea that he ran naked through the city streets!

Step 4: Verification

You might think that once you've had your lightbulb moment, the creative process is over. But you still need to review your idea. Does it solve the core problem you identified in the preparation phase? In the final stage of the process, it's important to use **critical-thinking** skills to evaluate and verify your idea. Critical thinking is a careful, focused analysis of something in order to understand it better.

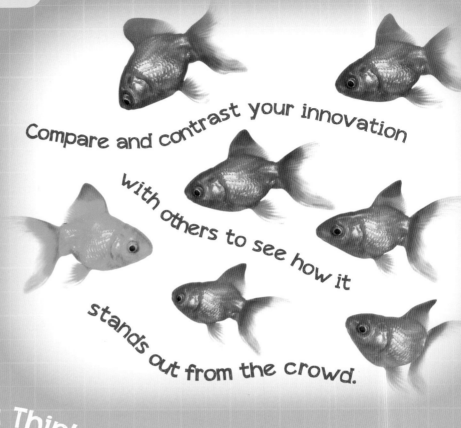

Compare and contrast your innovation with others to see how it stands out from the crowd.

Convergent Thinking

Fact Fact
Fact → ANSWER ← Fact
Fact Fact

Using Logic

Get Convergent

People use **convergent thinking** to analyze their ideas critically. Convergent thinking is the opposite of divergent thinking. It means applying rules to reach a single, correct answer to a problem. While there are no right or wrong answers when it comes to creativity, some solutions are more suitable or effective than others. Use the strategies on the next page to get convergent and put your ideas to the test.

Strategy	What to do	Example
Compare	Compare your idea or object with others to find the similarities. This helps you visualize your concept more clearly, see its relationship to others, and understand why it is important.	How is my lightbulb the same as other lightbulbs? It generates light. It uses electricity. It burns a filament to glow. It has the same shape.
Contrast	Compare your idea or object with others to highlight the differences. This helps you see the drawbacks and benefits of your design, and areas for improvement.	How is my lightbulb different from other lightbulbs? It uses a different filament. It lasts longer. It uses less energy. It costs less to produce.
Categorize	Identify the type of idea or object you have come up with and list other items in the same category. Grouping or clustering similar ideas together highlights uses and improvements you may not have considered.	Lightbulbs help people see in the dark. Other items in the same category include: candles fires glasses fireflies the Moon flashlights
Evaluate	Explain the value or worth of your idea or object in order to assess it. How will it help or hurt people? Who will use your innovation and how will you get it to them?	Lightbulbs allow people to work after dark. They reduce fires caused by candles and oil lamps. They are small, light, and affordable but are fragile to ship. They rely on electricity to work.

Refine, Revise, or Repeat

After you have examined your idea critically, you may decide that you only need to refine it, which means to improve it by making small changes. For example, you might want to modify the thickness or shape of your new lightbulb filament. You may find, however, that you need to change your materials or design more significantly. You might even decide to go back to the drawing board and start the creative process all over again! Thomas Edison tested—and rejected—thousands of designs before he created a lightbulb that was suitable for mass production.

Down to the Last Detail

Once you're satisfied with your idea, you need to elaborate on it. Use words, diagrams, **graphic organizers**, pictures, videos, maps, timelines, and models to explain your idea fully, fill in any gaps, and answer any questions that might arise. Elaborating on your idea by laying it out in different formats will help you see it from all angles and discover any flaws. It makes your idea real and allows people to fully understand and appreciate your creative innovation!

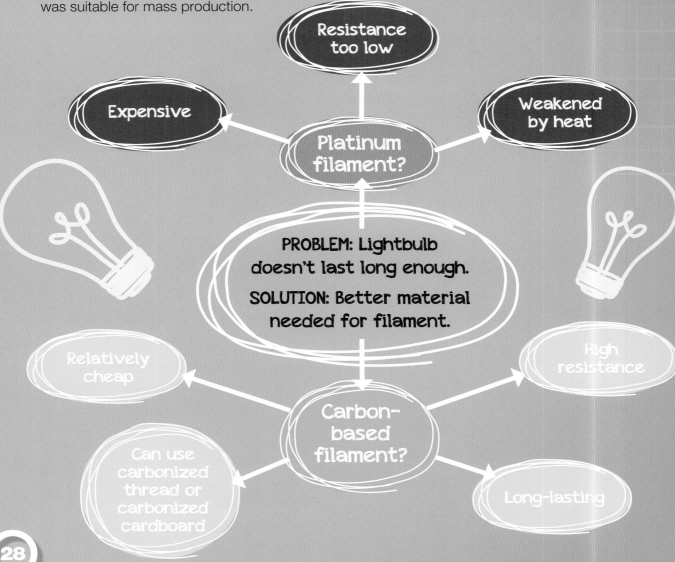

Resistance too low

Expensive

Weakened by heat

Platinum filament?

PROBLEM: Lightbulb doesn't last long enough.

SOLUTION: Better material needed for filament.

Relatively cheap

High resistance

Can use carbonized thread or carbonized cardboard

Carbon-based filament?

Long-lasting

SPOTLIGHT

Kenton Lee is changing the world—one step at a time. In 2007, the American was living in Kenya when he noticed that many children were wearing shoes that were too small for them. He founded the nonprofit organization Because International, and started designing shoes with adjustable parts that could grow with the kids. Lee and his team came up with 70 possible designs, then got critical and reduced the number to two practical models that best fit their criteria: the shoes had to be adjustable, durable, and light and compact for shipping. The team made 100 **prototypes**, had kids in Kenya test them for a year, then refined their design. Today, The Shoe That Grows adjusts five sizes, lasts at least five years, and is helping young people around the world put their best foot forward.

"I have not failed. I've just found 10,000 ways that won't work."

Thomas Edison

CHAPTER FOUR

GETTING UNSTUCK

A Mental Block?

Sometimes you might find that you just can't come up with an original thought or combine old ideas to create something new. You defined the problem, gathered data, and brainstormed solutions. You let the idea incubate and hoped for inspiration—but it just didn't happen. Now what do you do? Follow these tips to get unstuck and kick your creativity into gear.

Do ...

Do entertain all suggestions. Go back and review the ideas you rejected during the brainstorming phase. Why didn't they make the cut? Maybe you can tweak an idea and make it work after all.

Do let go of ideas that don't work. Sometimes you get set on an idea and don't want to change it—no matter how many dead ends it leads to. Be willing to start over if necessary.

Do learn from your mistakes. Examine why an idea or innovation failed. What parts of it could you keep or revise in your next attempt?

Do take risks. You might reject an idea because it seems illogical, impractical, or downright impossible. But look at the idea critically to see if you could make it happen. Some ideas are so crazy they just might work!

Do be patient. Prepare your mind to get creative, but don't try to force it. It can take months or even years to come up with a bright idea.

Google Glass has a hands-free display, similar to some mini computers and smartphones, that allows you to surf the Internet using voice commands.

Make It Your Own

Think of a time when you struggled to come up with a creative idea. Did you carefully consider all options and keep trying? Analyze your own performance and identify ways you could improve your creative-thinking skills in the future.

Don't ...

Don't be afraid to make mistakes. Even famous inventors didn't get it right the first time.

Don't aim for perfection or search for the single "right" answer to a problem. There is always more than one solution that will work.

Don't hesitate to imitate or build on the good work and bright ideas of others. You don't have to come up with an entirely original idea. You just have to put a new spin on it and make it your own.

Don't give up. You may have to return to the drawing board again and again before your idea is picture perfect.

Don't tell yourself that you're not creative. Negative thinking will hold you back and keep you from being the divergent, innovative, creative genius that you can be.

Creative Spaces

People do not create and innovate in a vacuum, which means that the world around you influences your innovations—and your ability to innovate! Everything you see, hear, smell, taste, and touch—from the color of your bedroom to the tidiness of your desk—can impact your creativity. If you're stuck for an idea, think inside the box and try changing the lighting, temperature, or other parts of your surroundings. Or think outside the box and go to a carnival, candy store, dog park, café, or any other place that gets your creative juices flowing. Try some of these tips to see what works for you when you're stuck for ideas!

Think about noise: Moderate levels of background noise, like you would hear in a coffee shop, can be helpful to spark creativity. Being a little distracted could help you generate lots of ideas. Loud environments, on the other hand, can make it hard to process information. Silence sharpens your focus, which helps people to concentrate—and could also be the key for creative thought, for some people!

Turn down the lights: Dim lighting makes you feel less **constrained** and free to take risks. Bright lighting is better for focused work.

Don't always tidy up: For some people, messy desks inspire creativity, while orderly desks promote more **conventional** thinking.

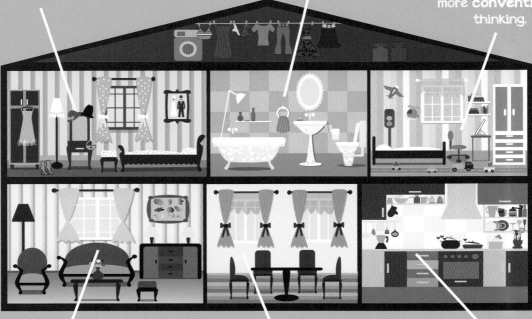

Go green: Studies show that the color green encourages creativity, possibly because it signals growth to the brain. Put a plant or green pillow in your room. Red, according to studies, helps us focus our attention on details but this might stop your creativity in its tracks.

Think big: Rooms with high ceilings and open spaces could encourage your mind to wander. Even better, going outside could broaden your horizons!

Check your temperature: A room that is too hot or too cold can stifle your creativity. Your energy will be spent cooling or warming your body instead of thinking up the next hot topic or cool innovation.

Maya Angelou always wrote in hotel rooms, even when she was close to home. The American author and poet woke early and checked in to a hotel each day. She insisted that all pictures were removed from the walls of her room so she would not be distracted by them. Angelou lay across the bed and wrote her memoirs and poems on legal pads. Then she went home and reviewed and edited her work each night.

"I insist that all things are taken off the walls. I don't want anything in there. I go into the room and I feel as if all my beliefs are suspended. Nothing holds me to anything. No milkmaids, no flowers, nothing. I just want to *feel...*"

Author *Maya Angelou*

People who prefer working alone

People who prefer working with others

67% **33%**

Although brainstorming can be more productive in teams, most Americans prefer to get creative alone.

Make It Your Own

Some schools are getting creative when it comes to education. They are setting up common learning areas, outdoor spaces, and other places that get students thinking outside the traditional classroom. In what type of learning environment are you most creative?

CHAPTER FIVE

INNOVATION IN ACTION

The Art of Creativity

Artists use creativity to imitate life and show beauty in new ways. Their colorful innovations come in a variety of forms. Some artists make inspiring paintings, drawings, sculptures, and other fine art. Authors create poems, books, and creative writing of all kinds. Songwriters combine sounds in new ways to create original music. Dancers, photographers, architects, cartoonists, quilters, filmmakers, performers, designers, and other artists have all got creativity down to a fine art.

The Big Picture

Artistic people use different forms to express themselves in different ways. They all follow a creative process of some kind, however. Studying artists and how they work can help us see the big picture. Michelangelo is considered one of the greatest artists of all time. During the Italian Renaissance, he created paintings and statues that have inspired awe and praise for centuries. But like all art, his masterpieces took preparation. Michelangelo carefully studied his subjects, built models, and planned and sketched his paintings. He burned most of his drawings shortly before his death. Why? Possibly so no one would see the demanding creative process behind his seemingly effortless art.

This challenge will get you thinking about how common items can be used in unusual ways.

Materials needed:

Pencil and paper, everyday objects

Challenge:

Lady Gaga is known for her unusual and creative fashion ideas as much as her music. The pop star has rocked a controversial meat dress, a telephone hat, and other unique styles. Brainstorm everyday items you could repurpose as clothing, shoes, and accessories for Gaga. Make sketches to prepare and plan an outfit for her. Then gather the items and try them on for size!

"I am a walking piece of art every day."

Lady Gaga

Make It Your Own

Think of the last time you created art. Maybe you took a cool selfie or drew a funny cartoon. Maybe you invented a new dance move or made a fearless fashion statement. What art did you make, and what did it say about you?

NOVELS ARE CREATIVE BY DEFINITION—THE WORD "NOVEL" MEANS SOMETHING THAT IS NEW AND DIFFERENT.

The Science of Creativity

You might think that science and divergent thinking don't mix. After all, science is all about following methods, taking careful measurements, and analyzing data, which all sounds pretty uncreative. It's true that scientists must be precise in their calculations, but successful scientists also look for different ways of finding solutions to problems. They question everything we know about the natural world and look for answers to all the things we don't understand. They conduct innovative experiments and use creative-thinking skills to interpret the results and find meaning in the data.

Hello, Dolly!

Some scientists lead the pack with their discoveries. In 1996, scientists in Scotland cloned the first mammal—a sheep named Dolly—from the cell of another adult sheep. **Cloning** may be useful for preserving endangered species.

SPOTLIGHT

Marie Curie was the first woman to win a Nobel Prize. She was also the first person to receive the prize in two different branches of science: physics and chemistry. Building on the work of physicist Henri Becquerel, Curie conducted new experiments on uranium rays. She later collaborated with her husband, Pierre, and together they discovered two highly **radioactive** elements, polonium and radium. Radioactive elements are unstable and break down easily, releasing a powerful and dangerous form of energy called radiation. Marie's pioneering research and creative thinking skills proved that radiation could be safely used to treat cancer.

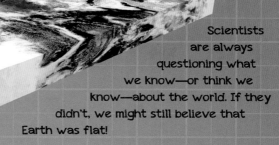

Scientists are always questioning what we know—or think we know—about the world. If they didn't, we might still believe that Earth was flat!

Under the Microscope

We can learn how to be creative by putting great scientists like Albert Einstein under the microscope. Einstein was a physicist who followed a creative process that combined unrelated concepts (such as energy, mass, and the speed of light) to make brilliant new theories and formulas. But Einstein didn't innovate from scratch. He built on the previous discoveries of Newton and other noted scientists, and he collaborated with other scientists of the time. And Einstein didn't put all his energy into his work. He also loved to play the violin and piano—and incubated some of his best ideas while doing so.

"The greatest scientists are artists as well."

Albert Einstein

Engineering Solutions

Engineers make the world go round—and find better, faster, and easier ways to make it happen. They apply scientific knowledge, math, and creative-thinking skills to innovate and solve problems. They invent new technologies such as cars, computers, robots, and cell phones that meet our needs and improve our everyday lives. And they have done so for thousands of years.

Building an Empire

The success of the Roman Empire was due in large part to the skill and creativity of its engineers. Roman engineers developed new materials and methods of construction that helped build up the empire and keep it standing. They invented concrete, a strong material that allowed them to construct large, sturdy buildings quickly and cheaply. Concrete takes the shape of the molds it is poured into, so Roman engineers could get more creative with the design of their buildings than ever before. The Romans also innovated the arch, a curved structure that supports heavy weight and allowed them to build theaters, arenas, and other massive buildings. The empire needed fresh water for its many fountains, public baths, and indoor plumbing—more water than its nearby streams and underground wells could provide. So Roman engineers got creative and designed aqueducts, huge bridges that used gravity to carry water long distances into cities and towns.

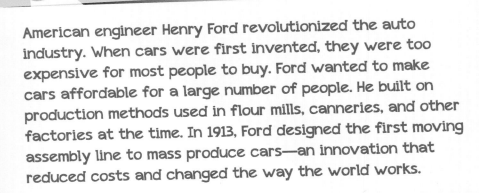

SPOTLIGHT

American engineer Henry Ford revolutionized the auto industry. When cars were first invented, they were too expensive for most people to buy. Ford wanted to make cars affordable for a large number of people. He built on production methods used in flour mills, canneries, and other factories at the time. In 1913, Ford designed the first moving assembly line to mass produce cars—an innovation that reduced costs and changed the way the world works.

Flying High

Today, engineers look to the past for inspiration. They don't reinvent the wheel, but they do reimagine the wheel and use their creative-thinking skills to make it better. Engineers strive to improve existing technologies. They also let their minds soar and come up with brand-new technologies. The Wright brothers invented the airplane in 1903. Since then, engineers have developed large passenger planes, stealthy warplanes, and jet aircraft that break the speed of sound. They have designed out-of-this-world spacecraft that rocket us to the Moon and beyond. Where will engineers take us next?

PLANES FLY HIGHER, FASTER, AND FARTHER THAN EVER BEFORE—UNTIL THE NEXT GREAT INNOVATIONS TAKE FLIGHT.

This chart ranks the top 20 engineering feats of the 1900s. What innovations might top the chart for the 21st century?

 1 **Electrification**

 2 **Automobile**

 3 **Airplane**

 4 **Water supply and distribution**

 5 **Electronics**

 6 **Radio and television**

 7 **Agriculture mechanization**

 8 **Computers**

 9 **Telephone**

 10 **Air conditioning and refrigeration**

 11 **Highways**

 12 **Spacecraft**

 13 **Internet**

 14 **Imaging**

 15 **Household appliances**

 16 **Health technologies**

 17 **Petroleum and petrochemical technologies**

 18 **Laser and fiber optics**

 19 **Nuclear technologies**

 20 **High-performance materials**

The Business of Innovation

Creativity is big business. Companies must constantly generate bigger, better, and brighter ideas to sell their products. They have to think quickly and creatively to stay three steps ahead of the competition. Businesses spend time and money trying to create products that will turn heads, make profits, and improve people's lives. In today's technology-driven world, the push for creativity is extremely important for technology companies.

The Big Apple

Technology companies like Apple, Microsoft, Google, Facebook, and IBM are in the business of innovation. They compete to develop new computers, smartphones, and other technologies that are faster, smaller, and better than the rest. Since Apple was formed in 1976, it has led the way in innovation. The company designs and launches sleek new devices, such as computers, iPods, iPads, and smartwatches, that are appealing and easy to use—and always the next big thing.

INNOVATION MEANS MONEY: IN 2015, APPLE WAS RANKED THE MOST PROFITABLE COMPANY OF THE YEAR BY *FORTUNE* MAGAZINE.

A 2015 survey asked top executives to rate companies around the world on their innovation. Half of the top ten spots went to tech companies—Apple, Google, Microsoft, Samsung, and Amazon. High-tech car companies—Tesla, Toyota, BMW, and Daimler—also took top spots. A pharmaceutical company called Gilead Sciences rounded out the top ten.

The Most Innovative Companies of 2015

1. Apple
2. Google
3. Tesla Motors
4. Microsoft Corp.
5. Samsung Group
6. Toyota
7. BMW
8. Gilead Sciences
9. Amazon
10. Daimler

The Drive to Succeed

Innovation also drives the auto industry. In the decades since the first Ford Model T rolled off the production line, companies have innovated to manufacture better, faster, safer, and more fuel-efficient cars and trucks. Today, the shift is toward more environmentally friendly vehicles, and Tesla Motors leads the charge. The company, named after pioneering engineer Nikola Tesla, designs, manufactures, and sells fully electric cars. An alternative to cars that burn gasoline—a nonrenewable resource—the cars run on batteries and are plugged in to recharge.

Tesla Motors' Model S runs on electricity not gasoline.

The Importance of Creativity to Economic Growth

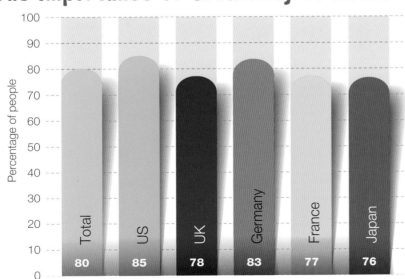

This graph shows the percentage of people in different countries who believe that creativity is key to driving economic growth.

	Percentage of people
Total	80
US	85
UK	78
Germany	83
France	77
Japan	76

CHAPTER SIX

CREATE YOUR FUTURE

Don't Stop the Music

You have now seen how to follow a creative process, get unstuck, and put innovation into action. But creativity does not stop when you put down the paintbrush or launch a new running shoe. Highly creative people don't make masterpieces or solve complex problems and then go back to their everyday lives. They always keep their minds open to new ideas and inspirations. They never stop observing, learning, questioning, and creating.

In Living Color

Follow these tips to live your life more creatively.

Find an environment where you can be creative, whether it's your messy bedroom or a hammock in your backyard. Choose a place that makes you happy—you're more creative when you're feeling positive.

Set aside time each day to be creative. You can kick around some new uses for soccer balls before the big game or cook up some creative rhymes at the grocery store.

Try new things. Taste new foods, listen to new music, and visit new places. Stepping outside your comfort zone can give you fresh ideas and new sources of inspiration.

Take up a hobby that uses creative-thinking skills. Start a science club, take an art class, or join a theater group.

Talk to people who are very different than you. Understanding other people's ideas and experiences helps you see problems—and solutions—from different perspectives.

Surround yourself with creative thinkers. They will inspire you to get into innovation and help you brainstorm when you're stuck.

Learn something new each day. Read a book on beekeepers or watch a YouTube video about sneezing in space. Learning unfamiliar things helps stretch your mind and prepares you to think creatively.

Keep your mind open and take an interest in everything around you. You never know what you'll see, hear, smell, taste, or touch—or how it will trigger your next great idea.

Reaching Creative Potential

A recent survey of adults in five countries shows that only one in four people think they're reaching their creative potential.

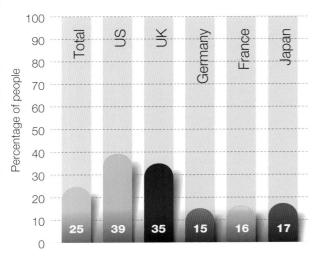

Percentage of people

Total	US	UK	Germany	France	Japan
25	39	35	15	16	17

Believes creative potential is being reached

Make It Your Own

Look at the graph below. How does your daily routine compare to that of some famously creative people? Are you most creative in the morning, afternoon, or evening? Do you take walks and other breaks to let your ideas incubate? Find out what works best for you—and then live your life creatively.

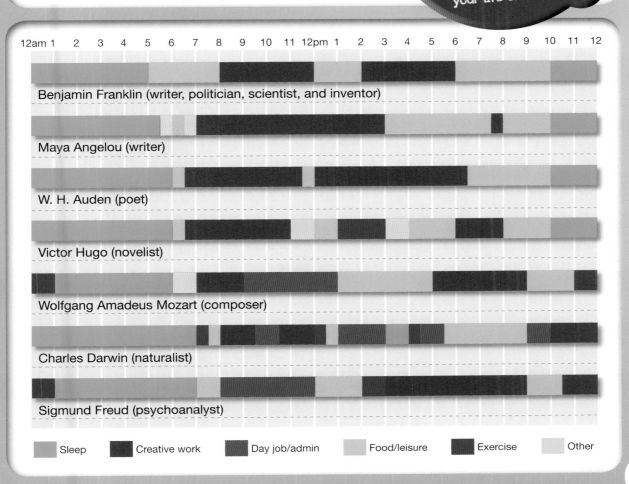

12am 1   2   3   4   5   6   7   8   9   10 11 12pm 1   2   3   4   5   6   7   8   9   10 11 12

Benjamin Franklin (writer, politician, scientist, and inventor)

Maya Angelou (writer)

W. H. Auden (poet)

Victor Hugo (novelist)

Wolfgang Amadeus Mozart (composer)

Charles Darwin (naturalist)

Sigmund Freud (psychoanalyst)

| Sleep | Creative work | Day job/admin | Food/leisure | Exercise | Other |

What Will They Think of Next?

You might think that everything that can be invented has already been invented. After all, today we have hoverboards, smartwatches, and even the turducken (roast chicken stuffed inside a duck and then stuffed inside a turkey). But there are always useful new things to innovate—we just haven't thought of them yet. There are also endless ways to change and improve existing technologies, making them bigger, better, smaller, faster, greener, safer, or smarter.

Improving Lives

Today, creative people are working on products and ideas that will benefit the human race. Engineers are driving the future with cars that can drive themselves. Scientists are studying teleportation—moving objects from one place to another without crossing the physical space between them—and other theories that once seemed like science fiction. But creativity is not limited to gadgets and innovations on the move. Creative people tell their truths through their writing, music, design, and other art forms. They search for creative solutions to all sorts of problems, such as how to clean our oceans, find renewable energy sources, and stop the spread of diseases that go viral faster than YouTube videos.

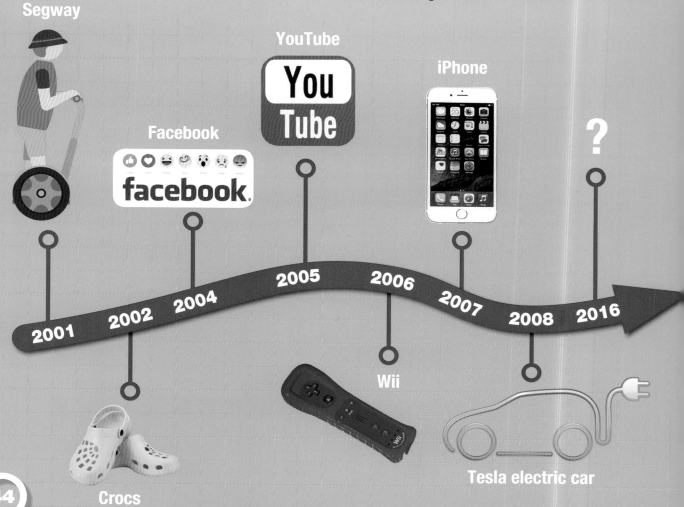

Segway

Facebook

YouTube

iPhone

?

2001 2002 2004 2005 2006 2007 2008 2016

Crocs

Wii

Tesla electric car

Create Your Future

Complex problems span the globe and demand innovative solutions. We have the technology to share our bright ideas with an international audience, connect and brainstorm with people around the world, and build on the work of great thinkers everywhere. Technology makes it easy to communicate our ideas, but it still takes hard work to achieve those lightbulb moments. You can train your brain and practice your skills to become an innovating machine—if you put your mind to it. What will you think of next?

> "The best way to predict your future is to create it."
> *U.S. President Abraham Lincoln*

GLOSSARY

brainstorming Quickly coming up with and recording ideas without judging them, often in a group

chemical elements Substances that appear naturally on Earth, which cannot be broken down into simpler substances

cloning Making an exact copy of a person, animal, or plant

collaborate To work together to create or achieve something

conscious The part of your mind you are aware of and which observes, analyzes, and makes decisions

constrained Held back or kept within certain limits

conventional Ordinary or traditional and accepted by most people

convergent thinking Applying rules to reach a single, correct answer to a problem

creativity Thinking in unusual or unexpected ways to make new connections and come up with ideas that are original and useful

criteria Things used as reasons for making decisions or judgments

critical thinking Careful, focused analysis of something in order to understand it better and determine its value

divergent thinking Coming up with many uncommon or unusual ideas and solutions to a problem

elaborate To work out an idea carefully and add details to it

filaments Thin wires inside lightbulbs that glow when electricity passes through them

genius hours Periods of time in school when students can explore topics of interest on their own

gifted Having exceptional talent or intellectual ability

graphic organizers Ways of showing visually how facts or ideas are connected; spider diagrams and mind maps are types of graphic organizers

illumination The stage of the creative process when you have a "lightbulb moment" or develop your best idea

imagination The ability to form a picture in your mind of things that are not real

incubation The stage of the creative process when you stop actively looking for answers and let ideas form in your mind

innovation Putting ideas into action and creating products or processes that are original and useful

mass production When goods are made in factories in large quantities

properties Characteristics or behaviors of a substance that may be observed when it undergoes a chemical change or reaction

prototypes Original or early models from which other products are developed or made

radioactive Describing something that gives off harmful particles called radiation

refine To improve something by making minor changes to it

subconscious The part of your mind you are not aware of and which stores all your thoughts, feelings, and memories

verification The stage of the creative process when you examine, check, and improve your idea to make sure it is an effective solution

volume The amount of space that something takes up

LEARNING MORE

Books

100 Inventions That Made History by DK Publishing. DK Children, 2014.

Biomimicry: Inventions Inspired by Nature by Dora Lee. Kids Can Press, 2011.

Creativity Unhinged: 120 Games for Kids to Spark Creative Thinking and Let Imaginations Run Wild by Marjorie Sarnat. Jr. Imagination, 2013.

Innovations in Communication by Cynthia O'Brien. Crabtree Publishing Company, 2016.

Kid Artists: True Tales of Childhood from Creative Legends by David Stabler. Quirk Books, 2016.

Websites

Biography.com
www.biography.com/people/groups/famous-inventors
Visit this website to read stories and watch videos about famous inventors.

Creativity Exercises
https://spark.adobe.com/blog/2016/05/31/10-exercises-to-spark-original-thinking-and-unleash-creativity/
Unleash your creativity and get unstuck with these ten exercises.

PBS Learning Media
http://bit.ly/29dD0LR
Watch a nine-minute Off Book video called *How to Be Creative* at this website.

Pinterest
www.pinterest.com/explore/teen-art-projects/
Browse this website for ideas to spark your creativity and inspire your innovations.

TED Talks
www.ted.com/playlists/11/the_creative_spark
Find out how to spark your creativity with this series of talks by creative people, including novelists and fashion designers.

INDEX

About the Author

Robin Johnson has been coloring outside the lines her whole life. She graduated from Queen's University with a degree in English and Film Studies, and she has now written more than 60 original children's books. When she's not getting creative at work, Robin builds castles in the sky with her engineering husband and their two best creations—sons Jeremy and Drew.